T

Chartered p...
illustrator Nick ...
to create a playful and uplifting guide
to positive thinking. Sam has spent many
years helping people take positive action
in their lives by making self-help strategies
engaging, practical and easy to use.

Read the psychologist's top tips
and integrate them into your
positive retirement. Enjoy the journey!

To:

With positive thoughts from:

The Ambitious Action Plan!

Retirement is when you reap the rewards of your working life. Make a list of the things that you would like to do, big and small, such as travelling to exotic destinations, creating works of art, conquering personal fears and spending more time with friends and family. The list should be courageous, challenging and most of all inspiring.

Kind Actions

Being of service to others
is a rewarding way to spend
your time. It fills you with
a sense of purpose and
raises self-esteem.

Think creatively about how you
can support your local community
and your family. Put this into action
and your energy levels and overall
happiness will increase.

Set the goal of doing at least
one act of kindness every day.

Do Less!

Starting your retirement
can be a daunting process.
Don't fall into the trap of
thinking that there is pressure
on you to be constantly
filling your time.

Recognise that you need
to concentrate on quality
not quantity and this
principle will encourage
you to organise your life with
those activities that are
really important.

Your Creative Side

Exercising creativity is
a fun, enjoyable and
therapeutic process.
Experiment with your
creative side by
indulging in the arts.

When you have a bad day being
creative will move your focus
away from yourself and limit
your ability to be negative.
Have several creative outlets
up your sleeve to stay positive!

Back To School

You are never too old to learn something new. Explore the potential of studying a new subject that excites you. Keeping your mind engaged and hungry for new information will add value to your life. Identify topics that excite you and try to further extend your enjoyment by sharing your newfound information with others in your community.

Green Therapy

Spending time in nature has been proved to boost your mood.

Making time every week to enjoy the natural world will create a sense of peace and contentment and provide the opportunity for you to gather your thoughts.

Notice at least one instance of natural beauty around you every day.

Get out into green space whenever possible.

Setting Goals

Setting goals is a useful process in streamlining and focusing your actions. Time is precious so it is important to use it to your advantage. Set daily, monthly and yearly goals to help you to get the most out of your time. This process will also help you to understand what is really important to you and will encourage you to be proactive in achieving what you want.

Well Defined Retirement

Most people focus on what they are retiring from rather than what they are retiring to.

Make sure that you look at your retirement as a process of moving forwards to an exciting new chapter in your life.

The way in which you define retirement will have an impact on your view of it, so make sure that it is positive.

Values

If we are not leading a life according to our values it is impossible to achieve true happiness.

However old we are, we all need constant reminders, so make a list of what you believe in and check whether or not your actions reflect them.

Your list might include family loyalty, honesty, laughter and caring for others.

Negative Triggers

Positive thinking is largely about how we react to negative situations.

During your retirement, try and turn negative experiences into positive ones by using the negative event as a trigger to do something positive.

Encourage yourself to learn from your experience by changing your actions in order to prevent the same thing from happening again.

Zen Activities

Happiness and self-fulfillment during your retirement is not only about filling your time with worthwhile and rewarding pursuits but also about how you meet your day-to-day tasks. Develop mindfulness and a physical awareness of everything that you do, not just the exciting activities. This will help you to stay in the present moment and become appreciative of the little things. Making dinner, drinking tea and having a shower are daily processes that all can be appreciated and cherished if your focus is in the right place!

The Simple Life

Complicated lifestyles are unnecessary during retirement. Simplify your life so that you spend less time managing your daily affairs and more time pursuing activities that are important to you. Often the fewer attachments we have, the greater the sense of freedom we are able to experience.
Some say 'simplicity is genius'!

Meditation

Meditation is an easy way to help you create a calm mind and body.

Spend 10 minutes every day with your eyes closed attentively focusing on one thing, for example your breathing. Notice tension leave your body every time your exhale and you will create an extra sense of peace.

The great thing about meditation is that it can be done at any time and in most places. You are meditating whenever your mind is solely focused on one thing to the exclusion of all others.

Gratitude

Focusing on what we are grateful for is a guaranteed way to feel positive.

Keep a journal of what you are grateful for in the present moment and also what you have been grateful for in the past.

Whenever you are feeling down, return to your book and remind yourself of the positives in your life.

Super Silliness

In modern life it is easy
to take ourselves too seriously.

We are prevented from truly
expressing ourselves by the fear
of failure and by worrying what
others will think of us.

During your retirement, invite
silliness into your life by
laughing more and indulging
in the extraordinary.
Set the simple goal of doing
something silly once a day.

No Regrets!

Most people don't regret the mistakes that they have made in their lives but they do regret the opportunities they didn't explore.

Seek different and varied experiences to widen your map of the world and to make retirement a magical experience.

Acceptance

When we are experiencing
stress and discomfort
it is often difficult to see
past our immediate sadness.

Recognise that all feelings are
transitory and will pass.

Accept the negative
and it will move out of
your focus and return you
to the positive more quickly.

Comfort Zone

Don't get bogged down
by comfort and familiarity.

See retirement as a challenge
to reinvent yourself.

Changing old patterns of
behaviour is possible;
it just takes courage
and willpower.

Get into the habit
of pushing outside
your comfort zone in
a small way every day!

People Power

Surrounding yourself with those who you love is a guaranteed way to ensure your retirement is positive.

Beyond this, also consider widening your social network through shared interest groups and community activities to increase your opportunities to meet interesting and exciting people.

Become A Mentor

Use your years of wisdom to guide and advise others. Helping others achieve their goals and work through their difficulties is time well spent.

Share your own personal successes and failures and no doubt you will inspire those around you.

The Pocket Psychologist™
Other Titles in the Series

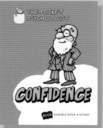

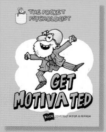
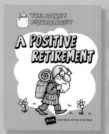

Published by Mindsport Ltd in 2012 - All rights reserved.
Printed in China

Mindsport Ltd
72 Prince Street, Bristol, BS1 4QD, United Kingdom
www.MyPositiveUniverse.com